MISGUIDED IN THE MAGNOLIA

A CLIMB THROUGH THE BRANCHES OF SELF-AWARENESS

EDWIN H. ADAMS

Copyright © 2018 By Edwin H. Adams.

All rights reserved. No portion of this book may be reproduced, stored in a retrieval system, or transmitted in any form or any means – electronic, mechanical, photocopy, recording, scanning or other – except for brief quotations in critical reviews or articles, without the prior written permission of the author.

Scripture quotations are from The New Oxford Annotated Bible, 4th Edition, The New Revised Standard Version (NRSV) with The Apocrypha.

ISBN: 9781977048875

Printed & Published in the USA.

❦ Created with Vellum

To Nancy and Matthew

The world changed forever the day you both came into my life. I love you with all my heart. Eternally Yours.

This above all: to thine own self be true...
~ Shakespeare

ABOUT THE AUTHOR

Edwin H. Adams is a change agent and an emerging thought leader in transformational development for people, organizations, teams, and businesses. This is Dr. Adams' first book.

Dr. Adams has over twenty years of experience working with high school, collegiate and professional sports teams, sports organizations, civic groups, professional membership associations, and corporations.

Learn more about
DisruptComfort.com

ACKNOWLEDGMENTS

Thank you, God. Your light shines through me.

I have to say a huge *thank you* to all the marvelous minds whose life experiences have contributed to my own growth over the years and consequently ended up in this book.

From my podcast and written interviews with some of today's top fitness, sports, and entrepreneurial leaders, I have had the distinct honor and privilege of speaking with many incredibly influential people. I have continued my conversations with most of them and have developed a network, a league, of truly extraordinary gentlemen. Thank you for your grace and patience as I continue to grow: *Johnny, Thomas, Marc, Austin, Mike, Dakota, Brock, Steven, Sil, Matthew, Joshua, Jason, Daniel, Phillip, Kyle, Michael, Dan, Matheus, Randy, Chad, James Scott, Micah, Whit, Lawrence, Maverick, Brian, Noah, Logan, Stephan, Shawn, Emerson, Adam, Glenn, Mitch, Bill, Guy, Walter, Tyler, Ryan, Mike, Gene, Russell, Terry, Bryant, Larry, Hap, Greg, David, Anthony, Matty, Rich, Kody, Jimmy, Gary, Kevin, Josh, Grandad, Christian, Cliff, Dad, Matt, Ralph, Tommy, Keith, Thaegen, and Nicolas Cole* ... to name a few.

And another huge *thank you* to my mentors in The John Maxwell Team and the Empowerment Mentoring Program. Roddy Galbraith, Paul Martinelli, Ed DeCosta, Christian Simpson, Deb Ingino, Mark Cole, and of course, my friend, John Maxwell, have consistently poured into my growth and development. For that, I am grateful and humbled.

Thank you, Beverly and Kathryn, for your grace, time, and talent in providing editorial support of my manuscript. And, finally, to my wife, Nancy, who is my biggest fan. Her relentless support of my vision is most appreciated and adored. Together, we have a beautiful and amazing son, Matthew, who is truly a gift from God. You both inspire me to be a better husband and father.

CONTENTS

PART I
A WORTHY IDEAL — 1

PART II
ON WHICH BRANCH ARE YOU? — 13

PART III
WHO IS GOING TO DO IT FOR YOU? — 25

PART IV
WHAT IS IT YOU REALLY WANT? — 37

PART V
WHAT IS REAL? — 49

PART VI
DOES EVERYONE SEE IT THAT WAY? — 61

PART VII
ARE YOU MILKING THIS? — 73

PART VIII
YOU ARE PERFECT JUST AS YOU ARE! — 83

PART IX
LOVE ALL LIFE, INCLUDING YOURSELF! — 93

PART X
IF IT'S WORTH HAVING, IT'S HARD TO GET — 105

PART XI
WHERE IS MY WHY? — 117

PART XII
COMING DOWN FROM THE BRANCHES — 129

EPILOGUE — 136

PART 1
A WORTHY IDEAL

ONE

A WORTHY IDEAL

When you reach the top, that's when the climb begins.
∼ Michael Caine

My childhood home was a natural playground. The trees and shrubbery around our house created the ideal backdrop for adventure and discovery. Yet, there was one tree that always captivated me...the great Magnolia tree in our front yard. It was one of the tallest trees on the property and was enveloped by a thick covering of the broadest leaves, deep green in color. And, once you pierced the outer layer of leaves, what remained was an intricate network of branches. The tree certainly appeared climbable: some branches within reach, others just out of reach. I could see the top though, and that's where I wanted to be.

> *Over several seasons, I eventually garnered enough strength and courage to reach the top of that tree. And it soon became a place I sought for solitude and escape. I had worked hard to get there. No one else had done what I was able to achieve – just me. Like a silent movie, I could see the entirety of the yard through flashes of reality in between the leaves. There was so much happening out there. What a great vantage point! Yet, I was too far up to participate in anything down below. What's more, no one knew I was present.*
>
> Excerpted from the John Maxwell Team's Leading-Edge Blog (JohnMaxwell-Team.com): Written by Dr. Edwin H. Adams

THAT IS where my journey began. At the top of a tree, in a very small space, stuck. I was comfortable. That was the goal as I believed it to be - just get to the top and everything else will be fine...I can stop after that. I no longer have to experience the pain of the ascent.

Back then, I did not truly know who I was, nor did I appreciate the potential that resided within me. I focused on being like other people. They were much more interesting, of course. They were more handsome, athletic, and popular. I did not believe I had value. So, I hid most of the time. Always sitting. Always watching. Fearful of any risk that might bring attention to my awkwardness. Carefully planning. Always finding the easy win. Never exploring my uniqueness.

The contrast is striking, is it not? I was unaware of my growth potential while sitting at the top of a tree that apparently *understood* it well. It is very natural for a Magnolia seed to germinate and to sprout. It is very natural for the seedling to grow into a little tree. And it is very natural for that tree to reach for the sky and to grow as tall as it possibly can. It does not take effort to grow. It grows because of what it is – a tree!

That seed may have been more comfortable sitting on the floor with nothing to do; but that is not what trees are supposed to do, is it? They are supposed to grow. And they are supposed to keep growing until they stop growing. And when they stop growing, they die.

As I look back at my life, I realize that all too often I have lived much like the seed lying on the floor than the seedling in the front yard of my childhood home! Not so much in later life, but certainly for vast stretches of my earlier life. If I was comfortable, I did not want to move.

The trouble with this mindset is that no one else is going to move you. In the top of that tree, no one even knew I was there! And as I sat on my perch, I was at the mercy of the tree. I moved where it moved. We all have to paddle our own canoe. If you sit back and rest, then by default you will begin to drift along with the flow instead of where you actually want to go. And water only ever flows downhill.

My friend and mentor, John Maxwell, says that everything worth having is uphill. And I think that most of us can recognize and accept that, when we stop and think about it. When we are comfortable, we do not spend much time thinking about what we want, where it is or how we can get it. Instead, we focus on what we do not want and worrying about losing what we have.

At the top of the tree where I sat as a young man, one thing was quite clear. That Magnolia tree had a very clear goal - to reach for the light. And that goal was relentlessly pursued every single day of its life. Little wonder it made such great progress and created such a unique hiding place for me.

If we all had such clear objectives and pursued them continually, I am sure we would astound ourselves with what we are capable of achieving.

I wonder why more people do not make such great progress in their lives? The statistics are staggeringly disappointing when you look at them. Only 5% of people ever reach financial independence. I read that most people die within seven years of retiring. Almost everyone is unhappy in their job and nearly everyone argues about money!

Is that all we have to look forward to after a lifetime of experience? What happened to all those hopes and dreams we had as a child? Where did that hope and wonder of the world go? What happened to that daily happiness that seemed to ooze out of us, infecting everyone around us. Why is true happiness so evasive for many and what do we have to do to get more of it?

Perhaps happiness is a childish fantasy, something that is not meant for grownups. As I reflect on that Magnolia tree from my childhood, I wonder if it was a happy young tree? Did it stop being happy when it reached a certain size and then become a miserable, pessimistic, know-it-all adult tree; only to finally become a gnarled, cantankerous old Magnolia tree? It may be silly to think of such questions about a tree. However, I find value in the metaphor. Happiness can never be pursued. Instead, it ensues from the realization of one's purpose.

In John Maxwell's best seller, *The 15 Invaluable Laws of Growth*, he tells a story that resonates with me. As a fortune teller read a man's fortune she says, "You'll be poor and miserable until you are 40 years old." "Then what happens?" asks the man with a glint of hope. "Then you get used to it!"

I love the prophetic brilliance in that story – not for everyone of course, but for many people. It is sad but oh so true, is it not?

Thucydides said, "The secret to happiness is freedom. And the secret to freedom is courage." Surely this applies to individuals just as much as it applies to races, communities, and nations. How many people do you know have the courage to pursue flexibility and freedom in their lives in an appropriate way? Do you think they are happy?

> *"For the gate is narrow and the road is hard that leads to life, and there are few who find it."*
> Matthew 7:14

Could that mean peace and happiness are indeed a scarce thing?

A great mentor of mine said that happiness is an *inside* job. It is not something you get from external circumstances or things. It is the result of what is going on inside your mind! He said that there is almost a 100% correlation between happiness and awareness or levels of consciousness. The more aware person can be happy completely detached from externals, while the unaware person is unhappy no matter what. Nothing you can do for them will make them happy.

Perhaps happiness is, as Earl Nightingale said, the progressive realization of a worthy ideal. If the tree from my childhood were capable of experiencing happiness in a tree-like way, I think it would be happiest when it was reaching and stretching and growing for the light – a worthy ideal, slowly but inexorably realized, in ever-greater degrees but never completed. However, I sat as a passenger on a branch. I was comfortable. My needs were met. I was safe. I was unseen. I did not have to take any risk. And all the while, the tree was reaching for the sky. I missed the hint.

Do you have a philosophy on life and happiness? How committed are you to this belief? Is it realistic? Is it logical? And most important of all, is it helping you? What a great question to ask yourself, "How's that working for you?" The answer to that single question can help you clearly see if your current actions, thoughts, feelings, habits, or mood are productive or not. If they are not, they must go!

Whatever your philosophy on happiness, taking responsibility for your growth and having the courage to face life is undoubtedly the best strategy for growth in every aspect of your being.

I hope in some small way this book can help you in that pursuit by giving you a formula for extracting more of the rich marrow of life. It works for everyone who embraces it and applies it.

Life is a wonderful adventure. You are already very good at it, but you can get better. Every effort you make to develop and to grow through your life experiences will inevitably be reflected in your experience of the world.

It certainly is true that we all get experience, but not all of us stop and think about what we can learn from these encounters. All too often we carry on banging our head against the same wall without realizing it is our own making. We do not have to bang our head against it. It may not even be there at all.

Wherever you are on your journey, whatever the circumstances of your life and however you feel about it, I want to reach out to you and to let you know that you are a wonderful human being capable of far more than you ever thought possible - your potential in life is limitless. You are perfectly imperfect, just like everyone else. You are no better than anyone else and no worse. And there is a wonderful life awaiting you beyond the terror barrier of your comfort zone.

THINK ABOUT IT

Nothing in this world can take the place of persistence. Talent will not; nothing is more common than unsuccessful men with talent. Genius will not; unrewarded genius is almost a proverb. Education will not; the world is full of educated derelicts. Persistence and determination alone are omnipotent. The slogan 'Press On!' has solved and always will solve the problems of the human race.

~ Calvin Coolidge

TAKE ACTION

- What decisions in life are you making right now, and how are they working for you?
- What would a dream life look like for you?
- If you knew you couldn't fail, what would you pursue?
- If you were to leave this world right now, would you be content with what you've done here and who you've become?
- When it's all over and someone is summing up your life and the kind of person you are, what do you think they would say?
- What would you like them to say?
- What personal assessments have you completed? (i.e. StrengthFinders, 16Personalities, etc.) What strengths do they identify within you? How might you begin acting from those platforms of strength?
- Write out the answers, or think about them, or better yet, discuss them with a loved one.

PART 2
ON WHICH BRANCH ARE YOU?

TWO

ON WHICH BRANCH ARE YOU?

If the highest aim of a captain were to preserve his ship, he would keep it in port forever.
  ~ Thomas Aquinas

I HAD an affinity for trees when I was young. I think it was because they were able to achieve an altitude that I could not. Instead of learning from their relentless pursuit, I remained envious. I believed the view would be better from the top than from my vantage point. I can remember praying for superhero powers in order to fly to such a height. In essence, I wanted the skill of climbing to high altitudes without having to work hard. How was I misguided in the Magnolia? From the top of that tree, I could see snapshots in time of what was happening around me. Though I saw much, it was limited in scope and duration through the outer protective layer under which I sat. My perception became clouded by the exact thing I sought for safety and comfort. So much may have been happening around me, yet the opacity of the leaves occluded my perspective.

I had created a barrier against the outside world. That view from the top is not the same as the view from lower branches, or even the ground. I was alone. My view, my perceptions, were filtered through the lens of my current existence and my past experiences. My truth was influenced by what I saw and experienced in solitude. Yet, authentic leadership (i.e., influence) is realized not through vision, but through connection. Connection demands proximity, not high-altitude observation.

Next to my Magnolia tree was an old brick garage. Inside the garage, my dad and brother created a makeshift gym. It was not fancy by any measure. But the shelter provided a year-round opportunity for a battle against gravity.

I remember hearing the old cast-iron weights crashing against the concrete as my brother lifted them incessantly with the goal of growing bigger and stronger. My dad and brother often spent quality time together in that cave, growing and learning together. And he even achieved some serious gains through his dedication. Because of his persistence, my brother became an incredible high school athlete. All the while, my father implored me to join them. Yet I sat stuck on a branch at the top of the tree. Comfortable. Doubtful. Wanting more, but not knowing how - not believing I could be like my brother. I wish I had at least tried.

Physical fitness has long been a dream for my identity. I was the tall, lanky kid in high school and received my share of bullying because of my awkwardness. I earned the nickname, "lucky legs"... *lucky they don't break* was the pun. I never believed I could do anything about it. No one else thought I could either, and they did not mind telling me. I simply did not believe in me. I was stuck on my branch of doubt. Academics came easy though; with all that time in solitude, books and study became my constant friends.

One of the biggest lessons and a really powerful learning experience for me happened in February 2012, at the age of 41.

My friend, Johnny, invited me to participate in a GoRuck Tough Challenge (*GoRuck.com*) in New Orleans, Louisiana, over Mardi Gras weekend. Beginning in City Park at 10 PM and continuing for 12.5 hours, Cadre Dan led our unruly crew of twelve people through a grueling series of trials and tribulations. We waded in water with alligators. We carried huge logs for miles. We scaled the parking garage of the Mercedes Benz Superdome with zero equipment. And we took turns leading our team through many other physical and mental challenges. We never stopped moving. I can remember asking myself over and over again, "What am I doing here? I am not worthy or capable of doing this level of physical exertion." The voice of fear echoed in my head. And then I would hear it, "Come on Ed, you've got this." A consistent and targeted message to me from my friend, Johnny. I'll never forget it. He knew my pain; but he saw my potential. Perhaps it is better stated this way: I am not who I think I am. I am not who you think I am. I am who I think you think I am.

During one of the toughest challenges I had ever faced, an interesting thing happened. My brain decided to continue when every muscle and joint in my body was telling me to quit. Having heard the message enough from my friend, I began to believe it myself. I was going to finish this challenge...and my body complied with that directive. I finished the challenge. For weeks and months afterward, even today, I feel elated. I risked failure; but I won. And I even have the battle scars to prove it - my badges of honor emblazoned on my skin. What's more, I had finally moved off of a branch on which I had been sitting for quite some time. I disrupted my comfort zone.

I realize now that I learned much more in life from those scars than from sitting on a tall branch in a tree. I had to give up my comfort zone in order to go up the side of a parking garage along with my team. They needed me, and I needed them. The GoRuck Tough Challenge was not a race of one, but a team of twelve working together over every obstacle placed in our path. My body grew through movement. My mind grew through leadership, and my spirit grew through pain. I was alive with hope atop a pillar of growth. Thank you, Johnny, for the consistent reminders even today.

It is true for all of us, is it not? We are designed for continual growth in all areas of our lives and all areas of our personality – body, mind and spirit. Sometimes it helps to understand where we are and who we are right now. It changes over time! So remembering who you may have been a long time ago may not be relevant today. Pausing long enough to ask for personal evaluations from others or perhaps taking a personality test or two to obtain some new perspectives on your strengths and uniqueness could shed some new light on today's reality. John Maxwell taught me that influence is highest form of leadership. And we influence and fascinate people with our strengths. Our weaknesses are not compelling; nor are they memorable. Find your strengths. Understand them. They are your unique power. Searching for them is a growth process.

And if we are not growing in a particular area of life, if we are not getting better, then we are getting worse! Nothing stands still. Everything is moving in one direction or the other. It is in a state of growth or in a state of stagnation. Scientists and theologians refer to these constant shifts in direction as ordered chaos.

Everything is perpetually changing. The world around us today is changing at a faster rate. The only way we can be comfortable in such a world is to learn to learn. We need to be able to constantly adapt and to grow. We need to constantly be able to learn, to unlearn, and to relearn!

I remember hearing a story of a speaker opening a presentation by walking on stage with a six-foot tall dinosaur. He set it down on the stage and then wrote 'RTC' in big letters on the flip chart. He then took a live, white mouse out of his briefcase and let it run from hand to hand for about thirty seconds. Looking-up at the audience he asked, "Who would have put money on this little guy outlasting this big guy 65 million years ago?" Then he turned to the board and said, "**R**esistant **T**o **C**hange!"

I have studied, coached, and taught professional leadership development for years, but that analogy stayed with me! It makes a great point, does it not? We are adaptive beings. We can assess and learn from our environments and change to fit them. In fact, adapting like this is more than just change.

I recently read that change is a different way of *doing*, whereas transformation is a different way of *being*. Evolution is perpetual transformation. I have always admired fitness professionals and top-ranked athletes for their physical transformations, as well as their mental ones. Each transformation begins with a belief that turns into an inferno, fueled by their limitless potential.

To thrive for sustained periods of time we need to be in a state of continual evolution.

This is difficult to do for many people. We do not like change, do we? As Tom Feltenstein said, "Change is good...You go first!"

THINK ABOUT IT

The problem with the world is the intelligent people are full of doubts and the stupid people are full of confidence.

~ Charles Bukowski

TAKE ACTION

- Where are you stuck in your life?
- Which particular fears are holding you back?
- Are there things you want, that you are not going after?
- When was the last time you did something you've never done before?
- Write out the answers, or think about them, or better yet, discuss them with a loved one.

PART 3
WHO IS GOING TO DO IT FOR YOU?

THREE

WHO IS GOING TO DO IT FOR YOU?

Responsibility is the price of freedom.
∼ Elbert Hubbard

IT IS funny how we had a feeling of invincibility when we were young. I am a pharmacist. And I have counseled many people, young and old, on the benefits and dangers associated with medication therapy for chronic illness. As any of my family members will tell you, I am the one pharmacist who hates medication, even the over-the-counter ones. I typically look for alternate means of treatment that do not require external chemical influence.

I remember a conversation I had with a client a few years ago. He was in his mid-to-late twenties and had committed to a physical transformation in the gym. Day in and day out, he worked his plan honed from the best practices he had researched from top fitness experts. But when it came to taking fitness supplements, he followed the advice of the other people in the gym. After all, if they were using them, then the supplements had to be safe and effective. If they were achieving new personal records and shattering their plateaus, then he needed to follow suit. My client would come to me and reiterate all the benefits and values that each one of the myriad supplements provided. He added that if he purchased said supplements from 'those guys,' he got a discount.

In the business, we call that bro-science. This word of mouth knowledge has always been a bur in the side of my scientific foundation of understanding into the body's chemistry. Needless to say, my client had spent hundreds of dollars on fitness supplements, expecting to see immediate outcomes in his physique transformation. Alas, no changes occurred. In addition, he experienced some adverse effects from taking higher than appropriate dosages of multiple tinctures and powders in order to get the desired outcome. Bigger, stronger, faster is not always the best strategy. When problems surfaced with those supplements, the bro-scientists made excuses and offered no solutions.

In helping my client alleviate some of the supplement toxicities and supporting him in developing a logical plan based on proper nutrition education and appropriate supplementation, I realized something valuable. The bro-scientist community that my client had aligned with had a certain solidarity. I soon remembered this when I was coaching someone who wanted to give up supplementation. We discussed all the benefits and eventually he took the plunge. He gave up supplements cold turkey and has not looked back. In our sessions that followed, an interesting dynamic appeared.

His relationship with the bro-scientist in his gym, the one in particular from whom he had purchased supplements, changed forever the moment he left that circle of influence.

It is a peculiar realization indeed when you begin to change and grow that the people around you, many of whom you love and who love you, do not like it!

As we discussed in the last chapter, no one really likes change – particularly change that happens to you, as opposed to change that you choose and drive yourself.

There is a certain dynamic to any club or group and the homeostasis is maintained by everyone *doing* and *being* the same. If someone goes and changes, it ruins it for everyone!

This is especially true of a "negative" type group – smoking, partying, irresponsible behavior, drug use, etc. If you change your life and stop going to the club every weekend you are, in essence, reminding your friends at the club that they should not be living this way. You are saying that you have the courage to change and they do not. Now things are awkward; they have a decision to make. They have to justify their choice to stay right where they are, and often they do this by criticizing you and your noble attempt at a better life! "Who do you think you are anyway? So, you are better than us now?"

I actually had a conversation with one of the bro-scientists from my client's gym who had spoken to their doctor about supplementation. He stated his doctor advised that he continue supplementation even at supra-therapeutic doses. How can you deceive yourself to that extent?

It is easy. We do not like change. And we do not like feeling bad about ourselves, so we will go to ridiculous extents to justify our thoughts, feelings and actions. We lie to ourselves.

What does this mean for our quest for success? It means that if you are going to change then you have to be ready for everything to change. Do not worry, it is a good thing; but being aware in advance is the antidote you need, because it hurts when people do not do what you expect them to.

It means that people you love as well as those you are indifferent about, will try to keep you stuck where you are, consciously or often unconsciously, because they do not understand, or they do not want change to happen to them. And some of them will accept the new you, but some will not.

Everyone in your life has some kind of vested unconscious desire for you to carry on as you are, so if you want change, it is solely up to you. We all have to take complete and utter responsibility for ourselves. Expecting others to do it for us, or even to be on board with us, just sets us up for disappointment.

This presents many problems for well-meaning parents. Years ago, my wife and I had many conversations about spoiling our son. We constantly evaluated whether or not we were neglecting him or empowering him. Were we preparing him for the future? Nancy and I still have those conversations today. And we watch for signs of our impact in the choices he makes. We cannot help it. But it is not about us!

Growing up, I remember having to make a critical decision about which college to attend. I received two scholarships, one from the state university and one from the university close to home. I had attended the nearby university two summers in a row and thoroughly enjoyed the small, hometown feel of the campus. My brother enrolled there five years earlier. The other scholarship came from a much larger university...the flagship university. That is where the prestige would be. That is where I needed to go, because my brother had not gone there. More importantly, everyone expected me to go to the big university.

So I did just that. I went to the flagship state university and quickly found myself to be a small fish in a very large pond. I struggled with the large class sizes. I did not have immediate access to the faculty members. As such, my grades faltered. I was miserable. The path ahead became less clear.

My mind raced for answers. How was I going to get out of

this mess? I vividly remember the overwhelming feeling when I had to call my mom and dad for advice. It was not a thought, it was an emotion – a powerful one. I did not want to disappoint them. I also recognized that it was time for me to take responsibility for this and to sort it out myself. I also realized at that moment that I had depended on my parents for far too long. I was a parent-sponsored, middle-class brat... and that had to change.

Taking responsibility is the first step of many different systems of help and change. If you believe that someone or something else is responsible for your growth, nothing is going to change. The world will continue to hold up the same merciless mirror, reflecting back the same life experiences until you acquiesce and agree to take the helm and chart your own course.

If you are not living the life you dream of, no one else is to blame. The responsibility to reach your potential is yours.

We have all been gifted with the ability to choose what to do in any and every moment. Our choices take us in different directions. But with that marvelous gift of free will comes the responsibility for the decisions we make.

Last year, I travelled to a major overseas city for some consulting work. There were many new sights and sounds, a new culture was around me. Similar faces doing their familiar things every day. The subway was the main mode of transportation. Again, same faces, taking the same seats, each day. It reminded me of an advertisement I had seen in another city a few years before. It was a television commercial of penguins shuffling onto the subway in vast numbers. They were all chanting, "Chop chop. Busy busy. Work work, penguin!"

When I was telling a colleague of my amusing memory, Einstein's quote came to mind, "Insanity is doing the same things over and over again and expecting different results."

I am sure the millions of people who commute into cities

around the world every single day are grateful for the opportunity. But I am equally certain that many dream of a bigger, better life. I wonder how many of them will wait until someone does it for them?

How long they will be waiting? A very long time.

THINK ABOUT IT

*You take your life in your own
hands and what happens?
A terrible thing, no one to blame!*

~ Erica Jong

TAKE ACTION

- Who do you depend on in your life?
- What do you depend on them for?
- Are there important things in your life that you are waiting for other people to deliver?
- What would it take for you to do what you are waiting for them to do?
- Write out the answers, or think about them, or better yet, discuss them with a loved one.

PART 4

WHAT IS IT YOU REALLY WANT?

FOUR

WHAT IS IT YOU REALLY WANT?

Goals that are casually set are freely abandoned at the first obstacle.
~ Zig Ziglar

BY REACHING the top of that Magnolia tree, I had achieved my goal. I did it. I did not ask for help from anyone; and I certainly did not ask for permission. But that is where my journey stopped. I reached the top and then sat down...for a long time.

And the GoRuck Challenge – I finished that too. I trained for it and completed it! But that is where my journey stopped. I crossed the finish line and then fell back into my comfort zone... for a long time.

Start, then stop - over and over. I had no plan for continual growth. As a young professional, I thoroughly enjoyed attending professional pharmacy meetings on a regional and national level. I would hear the most fascinating and inspiring content presented by some of the most captivating souls in the industry. Those meetings were not only uplifting, but they also offered me hope of a better tomorrow back home. Soon after returning home, though, my dreams of changing the world would fade. My comfort zone would consume me once again. I would return to mediocrity with my head hung low.

In my early days of executive coaching, I had a really bad habit of solving other people's problems. Something in their story resonated with some experience I had and abracadabra, I had their answer. Off they would go with their new-found piece of knowledge and wisdom; and eventually they would return with a failed attempt at *my* answer to *their* problem.

As I think back, I have realized it highlights a really important aspect of human nature. When it comes to someone else's goals, almost anything is too much trouble, or too difficult or inconvenient. When it comes to our own goals, things that we really want, there is almost no limit to the risks we will take, the energy we will invest, and the creativity we will draw upon to satisfy our heart's desires.

When we are focused on a goal that is important to us, everything in life is simpler. Decision-making is easy. Priorities are sorted in a heartbeat. Distractions do not stand a chance. And with a consistent plan of action, these growth opportunities can be repeated in perpetuity.

What is it that you want? What will stimulate your thoughts? What will cause you to launch and to push onward, even if you have not had your coffee yet?

There is an old saying, "No one washes a rental car!" It is true, is it not? If you do not own it, you just do not feel the same way about it. Do not let anyone else dictate your goals for you. You must find things that you want to pursue and do them! You are worth it. You deserve it, and as you progressively grow to the point where you achieve your goals and dreams, you will attain more of that elusive thing called happiness.

Earl Nightingale said, "Happiness is the progressive realization of the worthy ideal." My friend, Thomas, says it differently. "Trudge the road to your happy destiny." The key word there is, *trudge*.

Most people never ask the question - What do they want? I mean *really* want. They will list off the things that they *do not* want, but seem to get stuck with what they *do* want.

Paul Martinelli often says, "Most people say they want a lot more than they actually do and they settle for far less than they could easily get."

What are some of the things you truly want? Give yourself permission to stop and think about it. Do not include the things you need. There is far less motivational drive involved with needs. Think of the things that ignite your passion – the things that give you that surge of energy and a feeling of purpose. These are your worthy goals and dreams, and you do not have to settle for a life that excludes them. You just have to pinpoint what they actually are.

The desire to achieve or attain something really pulls us forward. It tempts us into growth. Going after something we do not actually know how to achieve (because we have not paved the way) forces us to tackle new situations and challenges in order to continue the process of growth in our lives. It forces us to take advantage of opportunities that we, perhaps, did not even see before, or discounted as being too risky. Going after something we want forces us to pick ourselves up after things go wrong and to try something else.

Indifference does none of these things. The things that we want can be large or small. They can take a few hours to achieve or a lifetime. The bigger the goal and the longer it takes to achieve, the more order it introduces into our lives.

For us to achieve anything meaningful, we need order and movement. One without the other does not really work, does it?

In James Allen's amazing book, *As a Man Thinketh*, there is a chapter about thought and purpose. At the beginning of this chapter, he reminds us, "Until thought is linked with purpose, there is no intelligent accomplishment."

The order that comes from a clear objective permeates every aspect of our life. Order to our thinking. Order to our actions. And order to our results. Order is heaven's first law.

When I talk to people about this, most of them can see that order comes from a clear direction, objective or compass bearing. What they truly struggle with is the answer to life's greatest question, "What is my purpose?"

Peter Drucker said it perfectly, "Only musicians, mathematicians, and a few early-maturing people, their numbers limited, know what they want to do from an early age. The rest of us have to find out."

As you embark upon this journey of "finding out" your life purpose, you are going to have to push past things that hold most people back from this journey.

Fear will try to creep in and tell you, "Oh, those are just pipedreams. You need to be grateful for what you have. Not everyone is marked for greatness. Just stay where you are. Do what has the least amount of risk." Essentially, all of these fear-based thoughts are attempts to convince you to settle for a life that is far less than you are capable. Is that what you want? Of course not.

You are going to have to face your fears. They will always be there. They will be waiting for your weakest moment, so they can tempt you to give up. But when you are willing to pull the mask off of fear, you will see it is powerless.

Yes, you might fall down. You might look foolish. You might make a huge mistake, but the other side of that looks like this:

- You will get back up.
- You will learn from mistakes.
- You will become an inspiration to others.

To me, that is worth the trials, the mistakes, the obstacles and even the temporary foolish moment.

Peter Drucker also said, "People who don't take risks generally make about two big mistakes a year. People who do take risks make about two big mistakes a year."

I would rather make my mistakes actively engaging in the pursuit of my goals and dreams. How about you?

THINK ABOUT IT

The problem with quoting people off the Internet is you can never actually be sure they said it.
~ Abraham Lincoln

TAKE ACTION

- When was the last time you sat down and listed all the things you want?
- What are the five most important things you would like to achieve?
- Which areas of your life are you really content with?
- Which areas of your life are you not content with?
- Write out the answers, or think about them, or better yet, discuss them with a loved one.

PART 5
WHAT IS REAL?

FIVE

WHAT IS REAL?

Get over it and look down upon it.
       ~ Walter Pierron

A FEW YEARS AGO, my son and I were traveling to San Diego as attendees of a dear friend's bachelor party. As this was quite a young crowd, I was the elder statesman of the group. Being with such an unruly crew of brethren I contemplated all the trouble that was about to ensue. I was not disappointed.

The idea was proposed for a skydiving excursion. I had never fallen freely out of a perfectly good airplane. This was going to be a significant challenge. Not only was I with a group of guys, but I was with my son and simply had to "man up." I put on a brave face, but inside, I was absolutely terrified. I think it was actually the ride up to 10,000 feet that was the worst. The anticipation of what was to come was overwhelming.

As an executive coach, I have studied human cognitive behavior across the spectrum of human development. Some of the most fascinating studies have come from examining the 'fears' with which babies are born. According to these studies, a baby comes programmed with just two responses: a fear response to loud noises and a fear response to the threat of falling. Looking out of the window of the skydiving airplane, I definitely experienced that primal fear instinct caused by the threat of falling.

The idea that we are born with just two fears provides a great deal of hope for the future of anyone who has suffered any kind of trauma that gets in the way of living their life and achieving the things they want to achieve.

At around eight to ten months of age, babies begin to understand 'object permanence.' Before this, if anything is in their awareness, it exists. When it is removed from their awareness, it ceases to exist. But after this stage, the idea that something is still in existence but just not there at that moment occurs. This leads to other trains of thought, like, "Where has mom gone? When will she be back?" This is connected to separation anxiety.

Another key developmental stages for children occurs with the development of the imagination. Every parent notices a difference in their child's interaction. They start making things up. They start lying! What is interesting about this stage is that fears can then originate from sources that cannot be seen. Enter monsters under the bed and things that go bump in the night!

During my childhood, my parents, brother, and I often spent summers on Lake Bruin in Louisiana. One of my parent's favorite activities was taking an evening boat ride to watch the sunset. One fateful evening we ventured out in the boat without checking the weather. Quite far from our camp I remember the wind whipping up suddenly and violently. The sky darkened, and a thunderous roar could be heard in the distance. Lightning began to dance across the sky. And soon, the rains came - large drops of rain that seemed to fall sideways with the power of the wind. The droplets stung my cheeks as my dad worked feverishly to orient the boat in the direction of our camp. In the chaos, I tried my best to understand all the variables that were rapidly changing. I could see the panic on mom and dad's faces. Shelter was nowhere to be found. I learned in that moment to fear this type of experience, not because I was experiencing it myself, but because everyone else was experiencing it too. And to this day, I still watch a thunderstorm roll in with awe, anticipation, and fear.

It is a normal part of a child's development to go through these different stages of fear. What is important is that they are transitory. As children learn to overcome these fears, they learn that they can deal with life. They can overcome challenges and state to themselves, 'That wasn't so bad after all!'

As adults though, if we are stuck with a certain irrational fear, it may (or may not) be a problem. If it is stopping us from getting what we want, then maybe it is a problem to be worked on and overcome.

There is an interesting thing about fear; we put total faith in it. We feel that something is going to happen, and we then trust that implicitly. We allow it to control our thinking, feelings and our actions, and therefore, our results.

Perhaps this is what Roosevelt was talking about in his inaugural address when he said, "The only thing we have to fear is fear itself."

If you think about it, it is interesting because the fear we experience does not exist anywhere except inside of us. You cannot point to it anywhere in the world other than the feelings, thinking, and sometimes even the symptoms you experience in your body. So, does that mean that fear is not real? If two people faced the same situation, one feels fear and the other does not, does that mean that fear is not real?

Fear is not to be confused with the danger. Make no mistake, danger is real. Busy roads are dangerous, and cars can kill you. In the right situation, panic can even be a very appropriate emotion. If you are in the road and there is a car coming for you, you should get out of the way! That is very different from sitting safely in your house panicking because of the cars out on the road. Experiencing a fear of cars when you are safe inside is an irrational fear. It is not real.

It sounds like a silly statement, but that is what we do when we fear the fear. A healthy concern, sensible caution, a few basic safety procedures and there is no need for the emotional response at all. Why use it then? Because we have learned to use it and now the tail is wagging the dog!

If you think about it, if fear is successful in its objective, you avoid the situation and never know if the fear was founded in the first place. Because you always experience the fear, you never find out what would happen if you just exercise basic caution without the emotion. The emotion will convince you of its necessity and if you comply, you will never know any different. Every time you engage avoidance because of fear, you are reinforcing the credibility of the fear.

If you are in the African Savanna and you see a lion, your body responds the same whether you actually see a lion or whether you just thought you saw a lion.

Imagine you are sitting at home staring blankly out the window. Suddenly just a single thought can pop into your head. Depending on the thought, a feeling of sadness or euphoria or anger can sweep through your body in an instant. Your pancreas begins to secrete hormones and your liver makes an enzyme that was not there just moments before. The blood flow around your body is altered.

And what was the cause of all these physiological changes? It was a single thought in your mind that does not exist anywhere else, and only then for a fleeting second.

Bruce Lipton talks about the effects of fear on the body and its ability to perform in a state of stress in his series on conscious parenting. He discusses the three key things that happened when we are in a state of fear:

- First, the cells of the body move from growth into protection. Blood moves from the viscera at the core of the body out to the extremities (muscles of the arms and legs) in order to engage in fight or to get ready for flight.
- Second, the immune system shuts down because there is no point using energy fighting a virus that may kill you in ten days if this lion could eat you in the next ten seconds.
- And third, the blood moves away from the fore brain to the hind brain so that instead of reason and logic you are better able to engage in reflexive behaviors. You lose your ability to think rationally when you are stressed.

Estimates put the figure at well over 90% for the things we fear but never actually happen. I once heard 'worry' described as chewing gum for the mind – it just gives it something to do but produces no meaningful results.

If a fear of loud noises or a fear of falling is holding you back from reaching your dreams, then you can take comfort in the fact that they have always been there. But if it is a fear of anything else, then that is something you have picked up along the way. You have learned to see in a certain way and that means you can unlearn and relearn in a more helpful and healthy way.

Put another way, there are beliefs about the world that you have acquired throughout your life. These beliefs are responsible for the emotions you are experiencing in response to events in the outside world (and your inside world). The feelings you experience, like doubt, fear and anxiety, stop you from doing things that you would otherwise like to do. If any of these things are stopping you from achieving your goals and dreams, then the underlying beliefs that are responsible need to go!

As I rolled out of the airplane with my tandem leader on my back, the most beautiful vista of a sun setting over the ocean came into view. The wind racing past my ears obscured all other sounds. My skin prickled under the pressure of gravity's pull, and then came a tremendous stopping force. The parachute was deployed, allowing for five more minutes of the most incredible views.

If I had let fear deny me that experience, I would have missed not only the incredible views, but also an opportunity for growth. My growth came from taking a risk and creating memories with my son. Thanks for the push, Matt.

THINK ABOUT IT

The most important kind of freedom is to be what you really are. You trade in your reality for a role. You give up your ability to feel, and in exchange, put on a mask.
~ Jim Morrison

TAKE ACTION

- What are you most afraid of?
- What are four other things that you are afraid of?
- Are any of these five fears holding you back from what you want to achieve?
- What would change in your life if you could overcome one or more of these fears?
- Write out the answers, or think about them, or better yet, discuss them with a loved one.

PART 6
DOES EVERYONE SEE IT THAT WAY?

SIX

DOES EVERYONE SEE IT THAT WAY?

Men are disturbed not by the things that happen to them, but by the views they take of them.
   ~ Epictetus

ONE OF THE most empowering exercises I have ever been a part of was called the *One Hundred People Technique*. I was working on an issue that I discussed with my colleague as part of a weekend training course. First of all, I described a problem in a little detail and described how I felt and the emotion that I experienced in the face of this problem. My colleague then asked me to imagine one hundred people, very similar to myself, who were facing the same challenge. "Would they all respond in the same way as you?" he asked. I thought about the question very briefly and said, "Yes. Of course they would, because that is the proper response to this type of challenge."

He answered with another question, "Well, what might some of the other possible ways of responding be?"

Eventually, and somewhat reluctantly, I said that some people may be even more angry and offended than I was.

He said, "Good! And what about some of the others?"

"Well, I guess some others might not be really bothered by this sort of thing."

"Good!" He said again, "What about some other responses?"

After a few minutes of this I came up with many different possible responses – anger, laughter, indifference, offended, pleased, scornful, sarcastic, guilty, etc.

He said, "And do you really believe that some people may respond in these different ways?"

I generally believe that they could.

Then he said, "Well, can you see then, that if it is possible for different people to respond in different ways to the same event, it cannot be the event that is responsible for the feeling. It must be something else. It must be the individual!"

It was a critical point for me because not only did I accept for the first time that it was something in me that was creating the emotions, but I also realized that I only discovered this by actually doing the exercise.

Do or do not. There is no try.
~ Master Yoda

You see, I had heard the experience explained by the lecture before we split up into pairs. I understood it, but I did not really get it. It was only when I took part in the exercise that I realized it was what was inside of me that was causing the problem, not something outside of me. It was not them at all. It was me.

It is a powerful realization indeed when you understand that your beliefs are the key to your emotions. It is what you believe about the event that causes the emotion, not the event itself. The way you see the world also comes from what you believe. Your perception of the world is a consequence of your acquired beliefs. And your beliefs are the result of a learning process, not a reflection of reality.

Some people see a situation in a certain way and they feel they only have one real option of how to proceed. As a result, they keep banging their head against the wall, over and over again, going around and around in circles, getting the same results.

But other people see this situation differently. They perceive a number of different options. They make different choices and they never experience the same challenges as the other person who is stuck.

Choice is a function of awareness.
~ Michael Beckwith

Over the past few years, I have been part of an Education for Ministries class hosted by St. Alban's Episcopal Church. Led by my priest and friend, Whit Stodghill, our group has discussed countless aspects of theology, scripture, and ministry. One of the many brilliant things Father Whit has shared with us over the years is that choice is a function of awareness. I have been humbled by the realization of my lack of awareness of the beliefs that have driven my choices for years. I have now awakened; it is empowering.

The more aware you are, the more options you perceive in any given situation. The more options you have, the higher the likelihood of picking the best one for you in that particular set of circumstances.

This is especially true in relationships. If you allow yourself to continually respond in the same way because you think you are right, then it can perpetuate the same vicious disagreements. You go around and around in angry circles, sometimes for years. It is not uncommon for people to cling to their sense of rightness, even long after the other party has passed away. The same emotions of anger or resentment rise up at the mere thought of the disagreement.

If you can find another way of seeing this – if you can search for other ways to respond – you will eventually bring about a different, better, healthier result.

And while it may be true that the application sits equally with both parties in the relationship, if one just cannot see things differently at this time, then the one with the greater awareness has the responsibility for moving things forward.

There is a lovely scene in the movie, *Night at the Museum*, when Ben Stiller's character is hitting the monkey in the face, and the monkey is hitting him back. And on and on it goes for some time. Up rides Teddy Roosevelt on his horse and says, "Larry, why are you hitting the monkey?" He says, "He started it!" And Teddy replies, "Larry, who has evolved?"

The responsibility sits with the person with a higher awareness.

Ramana Maharshi was an Indian mystic who reportedly reached enlightenment at a young age. He said that there are no levels of reality, only levels of experience of the individual.

Don't bother trying to change the world, the world you see doesn't even exist.
∼ Ramana Maharshi

He also said of people intent on saving the world or changing the world, "Don't bother trying to change the world because the world you see doesn't even exist."

The president of John Maxwell team and one of my Empowerment Mentors, Paul Martinelli, was the first person I heard talking about the idea of awareness. The more I think about it, the more I think it is the answer to everything.

So how do we gain a higher level of awareness? From experience. Everyone gets experience but not everyone grows at the same rate, do they? The experience must be evaluated in some way and insight needs to be gained. That insight needs to lead to change in the way we see the world and how we operate in it.

So, you could say that intention mixed with continually evaluated experience leads to a greater level of awareness over time.

THINK ABOUT IT

If I had a dollar for every time I got distracted ... man I'd love some ice cream right now.
∼ Unknown

TAKE ACTION

- What is holding you back from taking the next step toward your goal or your dream?
- What other options can you identify rather than not moving forward?
- Write out five different actions you could take, irrespective of whether or not you think they will work?
- Is there anyone you know who could deal with this differently? If so, what would they do?
- Write out the answers, or think about them, or better yet, discuss them with a loved one.

PART 7
ARE YOU MILKING THIS?

SEVEN

ARE YOU MILKING THIS?

Every action has its pleasures and its price.
　∼ Socrates

I REMEMBER a time in my early professional career when I was not selected for a job I really wanted. I had talked about it so much with all of my friends; and I was confident I was the best candidate for the position. I visualized myself working in that role and 'climbing up the ladder' within the company. In the end, however, I was not selected. I remember many sleepless nights filled with anxiety and a broken record of negative thoughts played in my head. I worried about what I would say and what others would think. But a dear confidant of mine called after hearing the news to remind me, "Once you stop worrying about what you haven't got, you can start enjoying what you have." That changed my perspective.

　　Why did I not spend time enjoying what I had? Part of it had to do with adjusting to a new reality from the position of my expectation. And that takes time.

But there is another aspect to it. I call it the poor me syndrome. This occurs when we first realize there is a definite benefit to sharing how unfortunate we have been in order to receive attention and sympathy. Being a victim can have good payoffs, after all. It also excuses you from the effort of trying, does it not?

I remember studying the treatment of tension headaches as part of my training in pharmacy school. The lecturer gave an example of one of her clients who was being treated for migraines. She asked the client, "What happens when you get one of your headaches?"

She explained the awful experience. "I have to go to bed and shut the curtains because I need absolute quiet. My husband has to come home early and feed the kids. He has to do their homework with them, make dinner, bathe them and put them to bed. I am unable to help in any way because I have to lie down and rest."

While I certainly do not want to offend people who suffer with debilitating migraines or any other type of similar conditions, is it possible that there are significant secondary gains with many of our complaints?

A counselor friend of mine says whenever anyone first discusses their problems with him, the first question he asks himself is how convenient is this? In other words, what are you getting out of this?

Dr. David Hawkins recommended putting a sign up on the mirror where you could see it every morning that reads, "Yours is the saddest story I have ever heard!"

There are two types of people in the world - life-giving people and life draining people. Life-giving people add value. They leave you a little bit better than you were when they found you. They tend to see the world from your perspective with you.

We don't seduce people by telling them how great we are; we seduce them by telling them how great they are.
   ~ Unknown

You may have heard the story of the lady who went to dinner with Mr. Gladstone one evening and Mr. Disraeli the next, both prominent English statesman.

She said, "After dinner with Mr. Gladstone, I thought he was the smartest person in England; but after dinner with Mr. Disraeli, I thought I was!"

What a difference between the two! Life-giving people make you feel better about yourself, but they also make you feel better about the world and everyone in it. They seem to lift everything and leave you with hope. They make you feel better about you!

Life draining people, on the other hand, tend to talk about themselves and they see the world from their perspective. You always feel worse when leaving the company of life draining people.

Most of us are not aware of our real motivations. For example, a woman can work hard, make money and declare she is doing it for her family. But the family never sees her, and when they do she seems angry and they feel like they cannot live up to her high expectations. They feel like a disappointment to her. Is she really doing it for the family? Is it possible there are hidden motives? She loves the attention and the respect. Maybe she enjoys not having to look after her own children.

On the other side of the coin, a woman could be without a job and because of a lack of finances, she might be forced to live on state benefits. Suffering at home all day, not enough money for a fancy car or expensive clothes or holidays to exotic places. But how convenient could that be?

If you do not have a job, you do not have to go in every day!

Of course, these are simple examples not meant to be illustrative of EVERYONE in those situations, but it is certainly true that the truth is seldom in the appearance of things. In order to move up and move on, we have to let go. If you are going to be mentally and emotionally healthy, you need to let go of the opportunities you have to continually seek pity and sympathy from everyone you meet! If you really want to have a great family life, you need to make it a priority and stop doing all the other things that prevent you from sharing experiences and making memories with your family. If you really want a job, you need to let go of all the upsides of not working and spend your time learning how to become a better job candidate.

Some of you, as you read through this chapter, will be offended at the mere suggestion that your misery has an upside whatsoever. How horrible of me to even come up with such an outlandish idea! And then you will seek out people to validate your feelings. You will tell them how offended you are. And you will explain again just how awful is your lot in life. Once again you will soak up whatever sympathy is available. Paul Martinelli describes the tendency of people to look for opportunities to be offended as one of the 'four pillars of drama' in his incredible teachings. Why would anyone possibly look to be offended? Simply because there is something in it for them.

Perhaps this is why Socrates said, "Know thyself." The unexamined life is not worth living. If you are really honest with yourself, how convenient are your challenges? Are you prepared to give up these conveniences in order to move forward with your life?

THINK ABOUT IT

Try to leave out the bit readers tend to skip!
~ Elmore Leonard

TAKE ACTION

- Where are you stuck in your life?
- Are there any upsides to being stuck?
- What would someone who knows you well say is the reason you are not moving on?
- Do you know anyone who is stuck in a key area of their life, who you know has significant advantages from staying stuck?
- Write out the answers, or think about them, or better yet, discuss them with a loved one.

PART 8
YOU ARE PERFECT JUST AS YOU ARE!

EIGHT

YOU ARE PERFECT JUST AS YOU ARE!

Be kind for everyone you meet is fighting a hard battle.
~ Socrates

EACH YEAR I attend a conference hosted by John Maxwell. There are several thousand people in attendance wanting to learn and to grow themselves, their communities, and their countries with the world-class leadership development content that John and his team provide. I have been very lucky to have the opportunity to travel extensively, working with people from all over the world. One of the things that becomes so obvious to me is this – the more people you meet, everyone is different, yet everyone is the same.

I believe we are all perfectly imperfect children of God, and no matter where you go or who you speak to, everyone is stepping forward courageously to face the human condition. One of my mentors said, "Having the courage to say yes to life is an incredible thing." The courage of a mother to risk her life to give birth to another life. The courage of a father to stand up to protect his family, his country, his way of life. The courage of every single one of us to stand up and say yes to our life experiences.

The only good is knowledge: and the only evil is ignorance.
∼ Socrates

We are not all meant to be star quarterbacks, nor beauty pageant queens. We are not all meant to be presidents or Mother Teresas.

Every single one of us is different, and every single one of us is perfect. Everyone struggles in some area of life and every single one of us is loved unconditionally.

If you look around, you see people doing their best. Socrates said man always chooses the good. Man can only choose the good. His only error is that he does not know what is for his own good. Everyone makes the best decision they can at the time.

This simple message has been said time and time again throughout history, "The only sin is ignorance."

If we accept the fact that we do what we do because we do not know better, then our path becomes pretty straight forward. How can we learn and grow so that we can make better decisions? How can we be just a little more enlightened?

Paul Martinelli often says, "The perfect curriculum for your growth is whatever lies in front of you right now."

I find this a very empowering train of thought.

- We are all perfectly imperfect.
- No one is any better than anyone else.
- No one is any worse than anyone else.
- We are all doing the best we can.
- We can all do better.

- We all have the opportunity to learn and grow.
- As we learn and grow we make better decisions.
- As we make better decisions our life improves.

We are ALL doing the best we can. It certainly makes pride seem empty and forgiveness a much more rational decision. *Forgive us our trespasses as we forgive those who trespass against us.*

We are all in it together, and we are all connected. There is a story about the word *Ubuntu*, which, to a certain African tribe means, "I am what I am because of who we all are."

It is said that an anthropologist who was studying the customs and lifestyle of this tribe spent a lot of time with the children. One particular day he decided to play a game with them. He knew they loved candy, so he made a trip to a neighboring town to buy some. He arranged quite a few pieces in a decorative basket and placed the prize at the base of a tree.

Excitedly, he called all the children together explaining that they were going to play a game and the winner would receive the prize, "When I shout 'now', everyone will run as fast as you can to the tree! The first one there wins the entire basket of candy."

Eager to participate, the children lined up and waited. As soon as the anthropologist yelled, "now!" all the children grabbed each other by the hand and began running as fast as they could toward the tree. Arriving at the same time, they divided the candy and began to enjoy the prize.

Slightly stunned, the anthropologists asked why they chose to all run together when the winner would have had all the candy to themselves.

"Ubuntu. How could one of us be happy when the others are sad?"

This philosophy and way of life speaks about our interconnectedness. You cannot exist as a human alone. Our choices affect others. Every day we are faced with a decision - we either choose to add value to another human life or to take it away. We are always making choices. Even the decision to do nothing, is still a decision.

Part of walking in awareness is understanding that we are responsible for the condition in which we leave others. How has our encounter affected them? What lasting impression have I left?

We often talk about leaving a legacy for future generations. Often, we are referring to finances or inheritance. But what about our daily legacy?

We are building a memorial to ourselves with every sentence, every text message, every email, every glance.

Realizing this certainly changes our perspective, does it not?

THINK ABOUT IT

These are my principles. If you don't like them, I have others.
∼ Groucho Marx

TAKE ACTION

- What areas of your life do not contain happiness?
- How do those areas affect your overall life?
- Do you know anyone who has similar issues who is not bothered by them at all or uses them as an advantage?
- How could it be true that your weaknesses are also your sensitivities?
- Write out the answers, or think about them, or better yet, discuss them with a loved one.

PART 9
LOVE ALL LIFE, INCLUDING YOURSELF!

NINE

LOVE ALL LIFE, INCLUDING YOURSELF!

There are two basic motivating forces; fear and love. When we are afraid, we pull back from life. When we love, we open to all that life has to offer with passion, excitement, and acceptance. We need to learn to love ourselves first, in all our glory and imperfections. If we cannot love ourselves, we cannot fully open our ability to love others or our potential to create.

∼ John Lennon

YOU HAVE FLAWS. I have flaws. We are not perfect. We are all going to make mistakes. It is simply part of the human process.

Shocking, right?

Is it not amazing that although we are fully aware of the fact that mistakes, detours, and unexpected results are part of the process, we often allow their arrival to stall our progress? Some of us get stuck for days or weeks, while others struggle with fear of failure to such a degree that it can derail our dreams indefinitely.

But why? Why do we get stuck?

In the closing chapters of *Think and Grow Rich*, Napoleon

Hill uncovers the basic fears that prevent us from attaining freedom and success:

- The fear of poverty.
- The fear of criticism.
- The fear of ill health.
- The fear of losing someone.
- The fear of old age.
- The fear of death.

These become core fears. They are learned. Depending on how we were raised or what we have experienced, these fears can affect us to a greater or lesser degree.

How do we combat fear? How do we push past the irrational and negative thought patterns that trigger survival mode and constrict our hope?

How do we live struggle free?

The good news is, there is a way to retrain your brain. It does not matter if you are eighteen or eighty, the negative thoughts that race through your mind can be recognized, rejected, and replaced. There can be a defiant power of the human spirt. You can create it.

How is this accomplished?

Fear is connected to our vision. It has to do with how we see things, and especially, how we see ourselves. For the most part, we see situations through our own filter or according to certain expectations. We do this automatically, without really thinking about it.

For example, five or six of us are at dinner and discussing real estate investing. The deeper we got into the conversation, the more you checked-out and disengaged.

Why? Because you are not an investor. Not only do you not invest in real estate, you have never owned a home in your life. In fact, your parents never owned a home either. So, instead of *leaning in* (which would be alignment), you might choose to *lean away*. It probably was not a conscious decision. You see, the left side of our brain (the part that is linear and rational) is constantly taking information from our experiences and connecting this information to our current reality in order to project probable outcomes. So if the entire table is talking about investing and you do not believe that is something attainable for you, it is likely the left side of your brain made the assumption that you will never need this information.

Hold it right there! What if investing becomes somehow connected to your future success? What if you are a late bloomer, but buying property is now vital to your life? Once you have this awareness (become awake to this truth) you have the power to change, to learn, to grow.

Maybe you will have to overcome some of the core fears Napoleon Hill discussed. Fear robs us of our power. While we are saying yes to our dreams and goals, fear is saying no.

Instead of allowing these fears to control us, it is up to us to:

- RECOGNIZE them.
- REJECT them.
- REPLACE them.

It is like being the bouncer of your brain. If there are negative thoughts and limiting belief systems in there, it is time to kick them out.

Let us go one level deeper and talk about *how* we kick out negative thoughts. It is certainly not by using willpower and choosing *not* to think negative thoughts. If you have ever attempted *not* think about something, you know how well that works.

If you have never tried it, go ahead and spend the next thirty seconds trying not to picture a purple zebra. Do not do it! No purple zebras!

Let me guess - They are galloping around in your head at full speed, right? I thought so.

Instead of attempting *not* to think negatively, the key is to *replace* fear and negative thoughts. We do this by reminding ourselves of who we are, what we are made of, and what is available to us.

You can use any positive affirmations you choose. The only requirement is that you believe what you are reading or declaring yourself.

Simple Bible scripture can be very useful. They can act as your daily promises. Here are a few I use:

> "I can do all things through him who strengthens me."
> —Phillipians 4:13

> "...for we walk by faith, not by sight."
> —2 Corinthians 5:7

> "I hereby command you: Be strong and courageous, do not be frightened or dismayed, for the Lord your God is with you wherever you go."
> —Joshua 1:9

Replace the lies fear is trying to tell you with the truth of who you really are! When your thought life is centered around faith in truth, you become a living, breathing container of hope. You actually begin to operate on a higher level. You begin to attract the things you desire because you are not allowing any interference from fear!

It is possible to form the habit of walking free from fear. It may take some practice, but the ability to boldly embrace who we are and live an authentic, courageous life is possible.

Remember, failure is not fatal, and it certainly is not final.

So, go ahead and try! Whether you fail or not, at least you are busy with living instead of standing on the sidelines of life, and that is something to be applauded!

In 2012, Sara Blakely became the youngest self-made billionaire. She was 41. She is the creator and founder of Spanks, a women's apparel product. The thing that impressed me most about her story was her recollection of sitting around the dinner table with her father every evening. He taught her the power of failing big and failing often. "Every evening he would ask me, 'So, what did you fail at today?' And if there were no failures, Dad would be disappointed."

Lack of failure means you are not stretching yourself outside your comfort zone.

I too remember dinner table directives from my father about exiting the comfort zone. I can still hear him yelling, "You're not supposed to be comfortable." He simply wanted me to take action. But for some reason, I believed the goal was to be comfortable – to just get by and to avoid the pain of failure. And to win the conversation and prove that I was in control, I would ignore the advice and respond in most disrespectful ways in order to protect my juvenile ego. In reflection, however, I must ask myself, "How was that working for me then? How is it working for me now?" You were right, Dad. Sorry.

By focusing on failing often and using it as a freeing and liberating exercise in the process of becoming, Sara understood that a lack of failure actually signified that she was not stretching herself far enough out of her comfort zone.

Each day we should strive to fully embrace life, and all the mess that it may bring. It is when we live to be more than we were yesterday, and chase after it without fear, that we begin to discover what we are made of and what we can become!

I encourage you to take risk, push against the imaginary barriers of life. Swim in the deep end! Choose to free-fall! Do not worry about failing. If you fail, it is really okay! You will get up. You will try again! You will make it!

THINK ABOUT IT

It took me 15 years to work out I had no talent for writing, but I couldn't give it up because by then I was too famous.
~ Robert Benchley

TAKE ACTION

- Who do you need to forgive?
- Why don't you forgive them?
- Where have you made mistakes in your own life?
- Why is it so hard for you to forgive yourself?
- What would it feel like to genuinely forgive yourself?
- Write out the answers, or think about them, or better yet, discuss them with a loved one.

PART 10
IF IT'S WORTH HAVING, IT'S HARD TO GET

TEN

IF IT'S WORTH HAVING, IT'S HARD TO GET

I can sum up the success of my life in seven words. Never give up. Never, never give up.
 ~ Winston Churchill

THE SPARK IS FUN, is it not? It is that moment of creation when you get permission to dream of a goal. That spark is usually accompanied by feelings of determination, optimism, passion and motivation.

Beginnings are exciting and energizing. They have the freshness of a blank page, and for most people, a new endeavor can be almost intoxicating. It is similar to the honeymoon phase of a relationship. And just like romantic relationships, substance is not built in the beginning. It is during the trials and the day to day encounters with each other that 'who we are inside' is established.

During this process, our dreams are either being fulfilled or forgotten. It happens one choice at a time, because it is *the process* that builds us into who we really are.

Success is developed daily, not in a day.
~ John Maxwell

Look around at your life. Think about your relationships, finances, and career. Now, dig deeper. Think about the things you are proud of, the things you have settled for, the things you would like to change.

Everything around you is a manifestation of your daily choices. You are in current, active possession of the kingdom you have created for yourself. Like it or not, you are the product of your choices.

The more I meditate on this, I realize that there is an art to living out our passion. It is an ebb and flow, a process of constant evolving and adapting.

If you are not happy with what you currently have, the answer then is to say yes to the fulfillment of your dreams and goals. In order to accomplish this, there really is a leveling of pride that takes place. In order to grow and to become all you can be, you will need to first take responsibility for who and WHERE you are.

Nothing good was ever born out of excuses, so if you have ever said things like, "This is how I was raised." or "I cannot help it. I am just doing what I know." I challenge you to ban these excuses from your life. You do not have to remain comfortable with terrible circumstances. You can take the sign off of your bathroom mirror because yours does not have to be the saddest story ever. It is up to you to make that decision.

One of the most liberating things you will ever do is to stand on the wreckage heap of your own broken promises, lies, masks, unfulfilled commitments, failures and mistakes and place your signature of ownership on the whole mess. It gives you a starting point, a place of accountability where you can say, "Yes, I am responsible for all of that, and now I am going to be responsible for all of *this!*" My superhero friend, Thomas, taught me this lesson. Thank you, Thomas.

Doing that is better than skydiving. It is risky, dangerous, wildly vulnerable, and 100% necessary if things are ever going to be any different in your life. Best of all, it is empowering.

We are who we choose to be. Every day. Every moment. We do not have to wait until church on Sunday or even tomorrow morning. We have the power to walk in the foolishness one minute and turn our entire life around the next. As soon as we realize we are doing something that is not in alignment with our best life, we have the power to turn it around. That decision can be made in an instant.

Right now. Or right now. Or right now. Any moment is the right moment to adjust your alignment. And once you decide, you give permission once again to the fulfillment of your dream, your goal and your purpose.

And how do my choices have anything to do with what level of success I am able to attain (and maintain) and my life?

I am glad you asked.

Success is merely the evidence of the level of discipline and commitment you have established for yourself. It is just like physical muscles are proof of your commitment to working out every day. Perseverance will ultimately solve most of your problems.

Star athletes do not become champions on the field. They are merely recognized there. They became a champion every time they said yes to their dream, got up early, finished their workout routine, and did what others were not willing to do in order to better themselves. Your success or failure is hidden in your daily routine. That is where it all happens.

Champions do not become champions in the ring, they are merely recognized there.

~ Joe Frazier

Former heavyweight champion, Joe Frazier, said "You can map out a fight plan, but when the action starts, it boils down to reflexes. That is where your road work shows. If you have cheated on that in the dark of the morning, you will get found out under the bright lights."

This is a perfect analogy for success in every area of our lives. It is all about what you do when no one is watching. It is about what you do to prepare. Do you walk in excellence? Do you operate in integrity? Are all of your choices bringing you closer to the fulfillment of your dream?

Let us go back to the chapter title, "If it's worth having, it's hard to get."

This statement is conflicting. The bottom line is this; any choice you make has hard attached to it:

- Choice #1: If you choose to live with intention and fulfill your destiny, it will be hard. Things will come against you. You will often have to go against the status quo. You may feel lonely at times and without encouragement. You will need self-discipline, commitment, and to constantly remind yourself that you can do this. You will have to give yourself pep talks and learn how to quickly realign yourself when you start to drift off course. Are all these things hard? Absolutely!
- Choice #2: If you choose to slack off, settle for less than you are capable of or become complacent, it will

be hard. You will constantly wonder what you could have achieved if you had only said yes to your dreams. You will regret the fact that you never stepped out of your comfort zone long enough to experience the thrill of success. It will be hard to look at your life one day and wonder what you could have been, if only you would have given yourself permission.

I am sure you will agree that both choices are hard. It is just that one comes with the promise of a fulfilled life and the ability to walk in freedom, while the other comes with disappointment and regret.

Both paths are hard. My advice to you? Choose your hard. Thank you, Thomas, Matt and Marc, for helping me understand mine.

THINK ABOUT IT

The greatest oak was once just a little nut who held its ground.
~ Anonymous

TAKE ACTION

- What is the difference between being stubborn and being committed?
- When you give up on something, how do you explain it to yourself? Do you identify good reasons why you are stopping?
- What is the upside of giving up in these areas?
- What is the downside of giving up in these areas?
- Write out the answers, or think about them, or better yet, discuss them with a loved one.

PART 11
WHERE IS MY WHY?

ELEVEN

WHERE IS MY WHY?

The two most important days of your life are the day you were born, and the day you find out why.
∼ Mark Twain

WE WERE all created with a purpose. There is an internal version of yourself, fully equipped with unique gifts, talents, and passions. This true version of yourself can either be suppressed, starved and ignored or nurtured and given the freedom to grow. The choice is yours.

You are not a carbon copy of anyone else. If you were, you would be dispensable. Anyone could fill your shoes and your purpose in life. But they absolutely cannot.

We complicate things, do we not? I think the fact that we are thinking and reasoning adults is sometimes our downfall, especially when it comes to finding our 'why.' You start out as children filled with wonder and optimism. Children say things like, "I want to fly. I want to touch the stars. I want to live underwater." Their sense of having the ability to become whatever they want has no boundaries. Limitations are learned later in life. As parents, it is our job to nurture our children's dreams and encourage them to follow their natural bent. There are numerous childhood development studies that outline the benefits of allowing your child to search, explore and follow their dreams.

The Bible provides some awe-inspiring insight into this way of thinking. Proverbs 18:16 assures us, "A man's gift will make room for him."

Your gift is that divine spark with which you were born. It is that certain something that you were created to explore. Your gift is connected to your purpose, your passion and ultimately, your ability to live a fulfilled life. It is all wrapped up in your big 'why'.

When you realize your gift and begin to fulfill your purpose, it does not matter how difficult the journey is. It does not matter how much time it takes to evolve or to become exactly who you are called to be. Money, education, and time invested in your purpose does not feel like a sacrifice to you, because it is what you are meant to do! There is an inner passion connected to your purpose!

German philosopher Friedrich Nietzsche said, "He who has a why to live for can bear almost any how."

How long? How difficult? How much will it cost me? How far will I have to go? How much more will I have to learn? How many more obstacles will I face? These things do not matter when you have your 'why!'

Scripture does not say, "Your education will make room for you." Now, I fully believe in educating yourself, but if education alone were the secret to a fulfilled life, then everyone with the degree would be living out the best version of themselves. Today's statistics on career fulfillment prove otherwise. Gallup surveys show that over 60% of the working population across all career tracks, educational levels and industries are "not engaged" or are "actively disengaged" from their work. It is not that we, as a whole, have lost our ability to connect with meaningful work. It is the fact that most of us are not living out our purpose. The work we are doing might be meaningful to the right person, but not to us!

When we actively suppress the part of our being that wants to dream and grow, we are settling for a life we were never meant to live. You can have all the education in the world, but if you are not actively reaching toward your individual purpose, something will always feel 'off.' It is that unsatisfied knowing on which many of us cannot put our finger.

The good news here is that your 'why' is right where you left it and you can pick it up at any moment. You have an internal compass that can still be accessed. It is the place where your dreams are still alive.

So, the question then is, "Where is my why and how do I find it?"

Your journey to your 'why' truly begins when you make the first decision in awareness. The moment you say to yourself, "I will give myself permission to find and live out my life purpose," the entire universe conspires together to bring it to pass. You move from darkness to light by one choice. The follow-up actions and steps you will make will reveal themselves along the way.

It begins with the decision to actively disengage from everyone else's explanations and allow yourself to fully access that inner child who was allowed to dream big.

Think about it. Do you remember the last time you woke up with the true sense of purpose, or have you been operating as a slave to the deadlines and constant flood of distractions offered up by the influence around you? It goes deeper than just focusing on positive thoughts and believing in yourself. You also have to agree to protect the vision and purpose that you have been given, even if it has not fully revealed itself yet.

It is as simple as this: the key to walking is to continue to walk. Once you decide to live out your purpose, you will naturally find yourself in positions where you will have opportunities to choose to nurture your dreams. You will also have opportunities to suppress them. It is a continual choice you are making with every step.

"But how will I know?"

This is where most people get stuck. Many of us are not used to accessing our internal compass. It seems 'new age' to nurture an unknown path. "What if I make a mistake? What if I fail?" That kind of thinking will have you right back in the grip of fear of the unknown, which allows us to settle for less than we were created to be.

The truth is, you do not have to know exactly how it will all come together, and I can promise you that you will not! Your biggest responsibility is to choose to say yes to your purpose every day without putting a cap on your dreams.

Everything else will come to you. Why? Because as you begin to say yes to your true purpose and give yourself permission to live free from the prison you have put yourself in, you will begin to see your goals and dreams with ever-increasing clarity. The fact that you *want* to see them is all it takes. The more you say yes, the more will be revealed. You have been stuck all this time because you made a decision to leave your dreams and goals behind. You lost your 'why' when you traded your purpose for something that seemed easier or more secure.

Compromise will always be there for you - so get used to that. But as you continue to live a life intent on fulfilling your purpose, the things you used to settle for will begin to sound more ridiculous.

It is like the guy who pushed against all odds to become the first entrepreneur in his family. He started out cutting his neighbor's lawn, and now ten years later he has seven crews who are responsible for all the golf course properties in his town. What would happen if someone walked up to him and offered him a secure management job with an hourly pay rate? If entrepreneurship is connected to his 'why' and he is living out his purpose, he would laugh at that offer. Sure, it may seem like less work, less responsibility and a guaranteed paycheck, but in reality, this man's passion is already attached to his business. He is fulfilled. He is continuing to grow. In fact, he has even provided jobs to young men in the area's community reentry program. These men served time in jail and now are receiving a second chance at life. This extra layer of fulfillment further connects this entrepreneur to his 'why.' Do you think he knew he would be helping change lives when he first felt that inner pull to start his own lawn service company? Of course not, but he had the courage to follow his inner compass. He decided to say yes. Congrats, Scott.

Where is your inner compass pointing you? If you choose to listen and continue to give yourself permission to live out your greatest purpose, you will find it, because it is already within you. Failure allows you to see a different path and a different opportunity. It is not a negative experience. Failure is our greatest teacher. So, fail first, fail fast, fail often. For it will not be in failing that your why is defined. It will be in your standing and stepping forward that your why is realized.

THINK ABOUT IT

Good judgement comes from experience. Experience comes from bad judgement.
∼ Will Rogers

TAKE ACTION

- Do you know why you are here?
- Are you happy to not know why you are here?
- Do you know anyone who passionately pursues their purpose?
- What difference does it make in their life?
- If you don't know your purpose, are you spending some time every day looking for it?
- Write out the answers, or think about them, or better yet, discuss them with a loved one.

PART 12
COMING DOWN FROM THE BRANCHES

TWELVE

COMING DOWN FROM THE BRANCHES

God doesn't require us to succeed. He only requires that you try.
∼ Mother Teresa

IF YOU HAVE REACHED this point in the book, I am guessing you are ready for the next marvelous chapter of your life. It is time for change, right? Another year on autopilot is just not an option anymore.

I used to lay in bed thinking to myself, "I wonder what I am capable of if I really threw myself into something with all my heart?"

And it was a comforting thought for a while. It took me away from the humdrum of my daily, disappointing existence; but inevitably I had to return at some point.

The interesting thing was that I somehow thought that the only requirement for my dream life to unfold was for me to be discovered. Someone would spot my genius and then everything would be all right! How can someone delude themselves to that extent?

Eventually I came to the realization that nothing is going to happen unless I make it happen. No one is going to discover you, no one is going to make it easy for you, no one is going to take away the pain. You have to do it for yourself.

For some people that might be bad news. But when you think about it, it means that your new life can begin any moment you choose. You are not waiting for anyone.

Your life may be dark and disappointing, but hope begins in the dark. You may be worried about failing. You may be concerned about being disappointed if things do not work out as you want it to. Well, you will be disappointed, because you will fail. But failure is temporary if you keep going. And what is the alternative? You are certainly doomed if you do not even try.

You may be worried about what other people will say. And it is true, you may well be in for ridicule and criticism from those who lack your courage not to settle for a stagnant life. But those who never made a mistake never tried anything new. And there is only one way to avoid criticism: do nothing, say nothing, and be nothing. And it is obvious where that will lead.

> Too many of us are not living our dreams because we are too busy living our fears.
> ~ Les Brown

You may berate yourself for not having started all this years ago, surely it is too late now. But no matter how old you are, you have the rest of your life ahead of you. It is pure folly not to go after a goal because of the amount of time it will take to achieve it, because the time is going to pass anyway!

Perhaps the very best time to begin would have been ten or

even twenty years ago. But you did not, so the best time is now. It is never too late to become what you could have been!

Why do we not take that chance? A colleague of mine, Les Brown, says that too many of us are not living our dreams because we are living our fears. (He also said that the tiger does not concern himself with the opinion of the sheep, which, although it does not fit here, I love it!)

We cannot afford to allow fear to hold us back. We have to find a way to go after our dreams, because if we do not, then we will spend our time working for someone else, building their dreams.

We do not need to be a genius and we do not need to be an overnight success. It does not matter how long it takes us, as long as we do not give up on our dreams. Never stop dreaming.

We need to find the motivation to keep moving forward, to go from one failure to the next with no loss of enthusiasm. If you cannot do it alone, find a tribe. My tribe is called 'the league of extraordinary gentlemen.' My friend, Johnny, often reminds me, *iron sharpens iron.*

The more we persist, the more we develop character. And character is ours to keep.

If we are going to be successful in living out our dream life, then we have to stand up straight and look life in the eye. We need to take part. We need to disrupt our comfort zone.

Some of my fondest childhood memories involved playing with my dog outside of our home after it had rained. I loved jumping barefoot into puddles or riding my bike as fast as possible through them. The sheer delight that I experienced is now beyond comprehension. I would have jumped in those puddles for hours if my parents had let me. But when they would drag me back in the house, soaked and cold, all I could do was cry because of the ruined experience.

How do we become so paralyzed and unadventurous in adult

life? Why are we so worried about messing up, making mistakes or appearing foolish?

As my mentor John Maxwell says, no one is good at anything the first time. So, if we are going to try new things, we need to create a disruption.

And that is okay! In fact, it is good!

As we take part in life, we learn and grow. But I am talking about more than just doing something different. That is change; but change is not enough. Change is *doing* something different; but transformation is *being* something different.

I am talking about being something different tomorrow than you are today.

But more than that, evolution is continual transformation, and that is what we need, continual growth. Continual change. Continual transformation. Continual evolution.

I believe that is why we are here, to experience life and to learn and grow from our experiences. To grow physically, mentally, and spiritually.

I adopted my mission in life from some mentors of mine several years ago – to be all that I can be for myself, my fellow man, and for God. Thank you, John and Whit. *Heaven on Earth*.

And I firmly believe that the only way any of us can do that, is by living life to the fullest – by disrupting our comfort zone.

I believe that is our responsibility to live. And we do not need to worry about doing it perfectly. We are responsible for the effort, not the result.

We cannot control a great deal about the world and all the other people in it, but we can control our own efforts. We can all do our best, and that is all it takes. You no longer have to peer at the world through the outer covering of your self-imposed limitations, atop the high branch of your own tree. Come down from your high-altitude perch and engage with the world that awaits you. We are better together, in communion and conversation - iron sharpening iron.

Good luck and may God bless you on your journey. Start now and go as far as you can see. When you get there, you will see how to go further. Help others do the same.

EPILOGUE

I believe in transformations. Not only the physical ones, but also the spiritual and mental ones ... whole person transformations that change trajectories of personal performance, growth, and ultimately, life. As a healthcare professional, I have seen amazing transformations in people's lives.

The logo on each chapter page represents all that I strive to personify and to mentor. It is comprised of a six-sided ring representing one of the most important aromatic hydrocarbons on the planet that fuels our economy, homes, planes, trains, and automobiles - the cyclohexane ring of benzene. To me, it represents the fuel for growth and a source of light. The 'Rx' symbol, associated with prescription medications, is the Latin abbreviation for 'recipe'. I stylized the abbreviation to represent each of our unique personal recipes. For it is in our unique nature that we find our God-given purpose. The triangle represents the three parts of our human existence: body, mind, and spirit. Mastery of each is a relentless pursuit. The outer circle encompassing them all represents our circle of influence: the people with whom we choose to surround ourselves and the environment in which we stand. Together, these symbols help to remind me of the priorities that are most important along a success pathway.

As a pharmacist, I have used medication recipes and formulations to support the enhancement of life through science. Science is only part of the solution. As spiritual beings, our minds are the source of all creativity, good, opportunity, and potential. I have developed my passions around finding recipes and formulations for success in those areas.

I joined The John Maxwell Team to use their world-class resources to further my personal development. On the journey, I've acquired a passion for coaching and mentoring others in doing the same.

If you are seeking a personal, business, or organizational transformation in any shape, form or fashion, I pledge my support to you. I support people, teams, associations, and businesses in optimizing human capacity, in removing barriers to human flourishing, and in finding subtle solutions to system problems that negatively impact the human condition. I help people get unstuck and achieve more.

Dr. Edwin H. Adams

Edwin.Adams@DisruptComfort.com
DisruptComfort.com

The Aesthetics of Leadership Podcast
On all major podcast outlets and at
AestheticsOfLeadership.com
Powered by Searchie.io

Made in the USA
Columbia, SC
13 July 2022